Hiding under His Wings

Susy Devasia

TRILOGY
A WHOLLY OWNED SUBSIDIARY OF **TBN**
PROFESSIONAL PUBLISHING MEETS POWERFUL PROMOTION

Trilogy Christian Publishers
A Wholly Owned Subsidiary of Trinity Broadcasting Network
2442 Michelle Drive
Tustin, CA 92780

Copyright © 2024 by Susy Devasia

Scripture quotations marked NIV are taken from the Holy Bible, New International Version®, NIV®. Copyright © 1973, 1978, 1984, 2011 by Biblica, Inc.TM Used by permission of Zondervan. All rights reserved worldwide. www.zondervan.com. The "NIV" and "New International Version" are trademarks registered in the United States Patent and Trademark Office by Biblica, Inc.TM

All rights reserved, including the right to reproduce this book or portions thereof in any form whatsoever.

For information, address Trilogy Christian Publishing

Rights Department, 2442 Michelle Drive, Tustin, CA 92780.

Trilogy Christian Publishing/ TBN and colophon are trademarks of Trinity Broadcasting Network.

For information about special discounts for bulk purchases, please contact Trilogy Christian Publishing.

Trilogy Disclaimer: The views and content expressed in this book are those of the author and may not necessarily reflect the views and doctrine of Trilogy Christian Publishing or the Trinity Broadcasting Network.

10 9 8 7 6 5 4 3 2 1

Library of Congress Cataloging-in-Publication Data is available.

IBSN 979-8-89333-590-3

IBSN 979-8-89333-591-0 (ebook)

Note From the Author

Dear readers,

My name is Susy, I am a firm believer in Jesus Christ and His words. Originally from India, I currently reside in the United States. Recently, I felt compelled to document some of my thoughts and experiences in a small book. Before proceeding, I prayed to the Holy Spirit for guidance and confirmation that this was His will.

Through my experiences, I have gained a deeper faith in Jesus and have been inspired to take action in accordance with His words. These actions have proven to be successful and have strengthened my faith even further.

I encourage you to read my book and believe

that you too can take action in accordance with Jesus' words. May God bless and protect you from any challenges that may come your way, including pandemics.

This book is primarily intended for Christians who read the Bible, since the Holy Bible is the source of every reference I make in this work. Yet, those who do not identify as Christian may also read this book and be inspired to accept Christ as their savior.. I sincerely hope and pray that this message may encourage everyone to seek refuge under His wings.

Jesus Compares His Protection to that of a Hen for Her Chicks

The Bible contains numerous passages that talk about God's wings and hiding under them. We can see that King David is the author of most of those verses. I believe David had this revelation from God and enjoyed the benefits of having shelter under God's wings. King Saul desperately wanted to kill David. That is when David came to the realization that he could find protection by hiding under God's wings. God the Almighty, who is the source of guidance, foresaw David's need and gave him this revelation. As a result of David's taking refuge under God's wings, even though Saul was the King of Israel, he could not find David to kill him.

Even though it has been mentioned many times in the Bible that we should hide under the wings of God, this advice won't be beneficial for us unless it becomes a revelation to us. For this reason, we must always meditate on the word of God. "Keep this Book of the Law always on your lips; meditate on it day and night, so that you may be careful to do everything written in it. Then you will be prosperous and successful." (Joshua 1:8. NIV).

Although I have read many times in different passages in the Bible, and heard many preachers preaching about hiding under God's wings, I have never grasped it in the way that I did when the Holy Spirit taught it to me. Then it appeared to me like it was carved into stone. My trust in my Lord increased.

In Matthew 23:37 (NIV) Jesus turned His face toward Jerusalem and said "Jerusalem, Jerusalem, you who kill the prophets and stone those sent to you, how often I have longed to gather your children together, as a hen gathers her chicks under her wings, and you were not willing." Jesus compared Himself to a hen keeping her babies under her wings for their safety and protection. The safest shelter in all the world for a hen's chicks is under her wings.

My Childhood Memories

Let me share one of my childhood memories with you that I have about hens and their chicks. I grew up in a village where there were many hens. These hens would rest for several days after laying eggs. After hens lay their eggs, my mother used to force those hens to sit and rest on those eggs for several days until they hatched. These eggs would break open and hatch roughly after 21 days. The hen was always aware that the chicks in the eggs were her offspring and that she should be sitting on top of them so they come out.

After birth, these chicks would walk closer to their mother. They would also walk around in the yard searching for food such as grain, bugs, worms, etc. Several birds, such as ravens, flew above them as the chicks walked around, hoping to swoop in on one of the chicks. The chicks wouldn't be able to see the threat since they didn't walk with their eyes constantly looking up. This could hve potentially caused trouble, but when their diligent and caring momma hen saw even a shadow of those birds flying around, she would make a noise to alert the chicks and gently open her wings so that each chick could hide underneath.

Even a day-old baby already knows what to do. They run fast to their mother for protection; I have frequently witnessed this. I have never seen a predator take a chick away from underneath the wings of its mother. The momma hen won't leave that protective spot either until the predator flies away ultimately dissatisfied. When I have witnessed this, I've noticed this momma hen glancing up to make sure that there was no more threat. None of the hens' chicks were lost to the adversary.

I once saw one of these chicks start walking away from the company of its mom and siblings to search for food on its own. While the baby chick was eating alone, those predatory birds flew down and quickly whisked it away. In this crucial moment, no matter how diligently or consistently the momma kept an eye on this chick, it became helpless. This baby chick was unprotected because the momma hen was unable to leave the other chicks who were already safely under her wings in order to go and recover her lost baby. But once the predator quickly swoops in and steals this one chick, the momma hen abandons all the other babies, starts wailing, and flees after the predator. She even tried to fly. But how can she? Due to the weight of her body, the momma hen couldn't fly too far. She went back to her other chicks with a grieving heart. Watching her concern for her chicks made me wonder how much more our heavenly Father is concerned about us and will keep us and protect us under His wings.

We should not be careless, saying that God will just take care of us. We have a huge part in our being taken care of, like walking with God, meditating on His words, loving Him, obeying Him, and praising and worshipping Him. Then He will definitely take care of us. Goodness and mercy will follow us. This advice is not just for King David, but for all of us. Psalms 23:6 (NIV) says, "Surely your goodness and love will follow me all the days of my life, and I will dwell in the house of the LORD forever." Our heart and life must be in alignment with God and His word.

Dear readers, I have seen such scenes many times in my life. This clearly demonstrates that we should be able to come and hide under our Lord's mighty wings willingly and wholeheartedly. Our father is always willing to keep us secret and safe. However, we should also be willing. I hear many people claiming that God will protect us and keep us under His wings, but some are getting carried away by the enemy, just like the chick was taken away by that bird. None of the chicks that stayed hidden under their mothers' wings were taken away. In a similar way, we must be deliberate in staying under the protection of God's wings to be out of all the dangers of this world.

In Matthew 23:37 (NIV), by looking at Jerusalem, Jesus said that even though He was willing to protect them, they were not willing to be protected. Dear children of God, we must be eager and willing to come under God's protection. Now, some of you might have started thinking, "Does God have wings"? I had the same question before I received revelation about God's wings.

Once, in my early Christian journey, I had a dream. In that dream, I saw Jesus coming down from Heaven with two huge wings. I was really happy to see Jesus in my dream, but I was confused about his wings. I had no idea at that point what the Bible was saying about God's wings. A few days later, I happened to read Psalms 63:7 (NIV), which says: "Because you are my help, I sing in the shadow of your wings." When I read this verse, my heart was filled with joy because of my dream. Besides that, the Bible talks about God's wings in many other Psalms. Psalms 91:1-4 (NIV) talks about God's wings and the benefits of those who take shelter under them.

Psalms 91:1-4 (NIV) says, "Whoever dwells in the shelter of the Most High, will rest in the shadow of the Almighty. I will say of the LORD, "He is my refuge and my fortress, my God in whom I trust." Surely he will save you from the fowler's snare and from the deadly pestilence. He will cover you with his feathers, and under his wings you will find refuge." I encourage you to read this whole psalm and meditate on it.

King David's Safety Under God's Wings

King Saul wanted to kill David out of his envy and jealousy of David. He tried to kill David many times. David was hiding in different places, like in caves and in the wilderness. But David was protected, as he was hiding under God's wings. We see this in Psalms 91 (NIV), which is below for you:

Whoever dwells in the shelter of the Most High

    will rest in the shadow of the Almighty.

I will say of the LORD, "He is my refuge and my fortress,

    my God, in whom I trust."

Surely he will save you

    from the fowler's snare

    and from the deadly pestilence.

He will cover you with his feathers,

    and under his wings you will find refuge;

    his faithfulness will be your shield and rampart.

You will not fear the terror of night,

    nor the arrow that flies by day,

nor the pestilence that stalks in the darkness,

    nor the plague that destroys at midday.

A thousand may fall at your side,

    ten thousand at your right hand,

    but it will not come near you.

You will only observe with your eyes

    and see the punishment of the wicked.

If you say, "The LORD is my refuge,"

    and you make the Most High your dwelling,

no harm will overtake you,

    no disaster will come near your tent.

For he will command his angels concerning you

    to guard you in all your ways;

they will lift you up in their hands,

    so that you will not strike your foot against a stone.

You will tread on the lion and the cobra;

    you will trample the great lion and the serpent.

"Because he loves me," says the LORD, "I will rescue him;

    I will protect him, for he acknowledges my name.

He will call on me, and I will answer him;

>I will be with him in trouble,

>I will deliver him and honor him.

With long life I will satisfy him

>and show him my salvation

According to this Psalms, we can be safe from the "fowler's snare" and from deadly plagues and calamities because God covers with His feathers. His faithfulness will be our shield. We don't have to be afraid of the enemy's arrows. Thousands may perish on our sides, but harm will not come near us. If you have faith in God, if He is your refuge, if you walk with God, then no harm will overtake you. For He will command His angels concerning you to guard you in all your ways. Psalms 91:15 (NIV) tells us that if we call on Him, he will answer us and be with us in trouble.

Even Absalom, David's own son, and many other nations tried to destroy David in many ways. The Bible tells us that David had victory everywhere and with everything since he was completely hiding under God's wings. No adversary could defeat him. Anyone who walks closer to God can always remain in the safety of His shadow. Only a person who has personally experienced God's protection in all circumstances is able to write a psalm like Psalms 91. Psalms 91 (NIV) has always been in the mouth of every Christian since COVID began; but do we believe it wholeheartedly? If the answer is yes, then we should let it reflect in our daily lives. "Believing in passages such as Psalms 91 should encourage us to act in ways that reflect our faith. We should actively seek to follow these verses and remember to take refuge in the Lord."

In all our circumstances and in our daily lives, Psalms 91 is significant. "We should remember the teaching of Psalms 91 as we see the influence of evil in the world around us."

God gave me the revelation of hens and their chicks before COVID started. I honestly lived every day by that revelation and believed in it. I completely placed myself, my family, and everything God gave me under His wings. Thus, I knew He would never allow my enemies to take over my life if I hid everything under His wings.

I felt really secure as a result of this experience. If King David was safe and secure by finding shelter under His wings, then my family and I would be too, since He is a righteous God. God doesn't show any partiality; he considers only those who trust in Him, adore Him, submit to Him, and have faith in Him. We must approach him eagerly if we want to walk under his shadow. We must continually walk closer to Him, so that we can be under the shadow of His wings. It should not be when something tragic like a pandemic hits us, but daily.

Psalms 57:1 (NIV) says, "Have mercy on me, my God, have mercy on me, for in you I take refuge. I will take refuge in the shadow of your wings until the disaster has passed." According to this verse, when we hide under His wings, God will keep us safe from our mortal enemies.

My Revelation of Psalms 91

Let me share a youthful memory of mine with you all. I had a friend who was significantly taller than me. She would walk faster than I did when we went outside because her legs were longer than mine. I used to hold onto her hands, especially when it was sunny outside, to walk in her shadow to stay cool. I did not really enjoy Bombay's sweltering heat. Whenever I read Psalms 91, this memory comes to mind.

One or two years before COVID started, God told me something. He told me to make Psalms 91 my own. So, to do that, I substituted all those "you" and "yours" in the verses with "me" and "mine". After I did that, Psalms 91 became my own, and it was highly powerful. All those sincere words that

I spoke to my Lord came from the bottom of my heart. My faith was greatly strengthened by this experience. I was able to withstand COVID because I made this psalm my own, and because I took refuge under God's wings.

Decision Not to Take the COVID Vaccine

I chose not to receive the COVID vaccination. I asked myself, "How can I take the vaccination to stop this evil (COVID) if I take Psalms 91 as my own and pray that Psalms?" When I say a thousand will fall at my side and 10,000 will fall at my right hand, as it does in the Bible (which happened during COVID), how can I depend on a man-made vaccination? Since I am over 65 years old with diabetes and hypertension, I could have taken the vaccination when COVID started spreading. The vaccination was available in the U.S. by the end of 2020. But I put my trust in my Lord and His word. I was able to put more faith in Him than the vaccine. I wasn't afraid of death. I was instead confident that because my family and I are under God's wings, this pandemic would not affect us in any way. Even if I were to have caught the virus, I felt that I wouldn't perish. Instead, I was going to live and glorify my Lord.

And if I had died, I would have faced death and said, "Where, O death, is your victory? Where, O death, is your sting? (1 Corinthians 15:55, NIV). I would have joyfully gone to that glorious heaven to be with my Savior! I spent four and a half months in India beginning in October 2021. I attended four weddings while I was there. I wore a mask on my face every time I left the house because of the law and because of my care for other people. Even still, I had to go without a mask in order to get food at the wedding feast. I am mentioning this to explain my Lord's great faithfulness in allowing me to stay well during this time.

I've since then heard that an Indian doctor from the U.S. passed away while he was in India after receiving two Pfizer vaccinations in the U.S. Dear Christian brothers and sisters, we must understand that our lives are in the hands of our Lord, our Creator, but not in the hands of COVID. God has already written an expiration date for every one of us, even before we were born into this world. No one will be able to remove us from the face of the earth until that time comes. So, be confident that His wings will shelter you until your time comes.

Ultimately, no matter what we do, when the time comes for us to leave this earth, we will. You will definitely have a death date if you have a birth date; it is certain. So why should we be overly concerned about this disease? I can only advise you not to be afraid of anything, including the plague. The Bible claims that all forces, including angels, are under the control of our Lord; therefore, we must understand that none of them can even move unless our God allows them to. 1 Peter 3:22 (NIV) tells us that it is Jesus Christ "who has gone into heaven and is at God's right hand—with angels, authorities, and powers in submission to him."

So, I humbly request that you all trust in the

Lord Jesus Christ. He is the only one who is trustworthy. If you trust Him completely, He won't let you down. Therefore, deliberately come and hide under His wings, like King David did. He will not let you go. He will never let the enemy see you.

Eventually, there will always be more serious diseases, plagues, and trials that life makes us go through. We must prepare ourselves for difficult times. That is the reason I am writing this small book. I want every believer to hide under God's wings before the next trial of life.

The Power of Jesus' Blood

Even though we see the Egyptians in the Bible were perishing from pandemics or plagues, the Israelites in Egypt were safe under the blood of a sacrificed animal. How much safer are we if Jesus' priceless, holy blood is put on our doors, when the Israelites were safe behind the door with the blood of an animal on it? I drew a figurative circle in the spiritual realm around my household and applied the holy blood of Jesus Christ to all of its entrances.

Our God is faithful. He will definitely honor our acts when we have intense faith in him. I would not say that this implies that we should disregard governmental regulations. Absolutely, I wore a mask. Since the immunization was optional, I chose not to receive it. The government left that up to us. Thus, I had the option to decline, even though they encouraged me to take it.

"Let me share another one of my experiences about victory in Jesus Christ. When Bill Clinton was our president, I thought all the Democrats who stood with President Clinton would say, "We won; we have the victory." If a political party could boast of their victory, why couldn't I say, "I am victorious, as my Jesus won victory over the enemy?" As Colossians 2:15 (NIV) says, "And having disarmed the powers and authorities, he made a public spectacle of them, triumphing over them by the cross." Since then, I started believing and saying that I am victorious, because my Jesus is victorious. I am in the victorious army of Jesus Christ.

If we say anything in faith according to the Word of God and His will, Jesus Christ will say "Amen" and sign His name!

Dear brothers and sisters in Christ, we do not need to be afraid of the evil one. He is the one who has been defeated. He was overcome by our Lord Jesus according to Colossians 2:14–15 (NIV).

Satan is a defeated foe. We have to believe we are victorious as our Lord is when we place our faith and trust in Him.

I did one more thing at the beginning of COVID in the U.S. Figuratively, by faith in my prayer, I applied the holy blood of Jesus to my doors and doorposts. I even drew a circle around my city spiritually and asked for God's protection in prayer. I applied Jesus' blood to my life by choosing to trust in Him.

One day, I asked my physician about my city's COVID condition. "It's not much; perhaps everyone had their shots," he said. "No," I replied, "It's the power of prayer." I couldn't even hear the sirens of ambulances on the road more than usual. My Lord kept my city safe. Some of the townspeople got COVID, but it was relatively mild.

The blood of Jesus is much stronger and more effective than any vaccination. Thank you, Jesus.

Getting Familiar with the Holy Spirit, the Third Person of the Trinity

One day, our Lord will return. Before then, we need to increase our faith in Christ. Without the shield of faith mentioned in Ephesians 6: 14-17 (NIV)) , we cannot resist the evil one. Without holiness, we will not be taken to heaven. We have to be dedicated and faithful to our holy heavenly Father. Our God is faithful. Our God is a good God. The problem is that we don't trust Him as much as He wants us to. We don't trust Him because we don't know Him and His words; His personality and character. We know that we can trust Him and His words because Christ is not a man that lies. He is the truth. We have to commune with the Holy Spirit. He is our helper and counselor. Jesus sent Him to give us help. Many Christians don't even know Him. They only talk to Father and Son.

The Holy Spirit is with all believers and He walks with us. Unfortunately, we often ignore Him. He grieves as we ignore Him. The Holy Spirit is our helper, our teacher, our counselor, our guide, and our guard. We have to actively turn to Him in our daily lives. Even to understand the Word of God, we need to completely depend on the Holy Spirit. He can take us deeper into the Word of God. Jesus said that when the Holy Spirit comes, He will teach us and bring things to our remembrance. The Holy Spirit will take us closer to Jesus. He will give us revelation of the Bible and the future. He will give us revelations to live in victory.

Christ is not a man who would lie; therefore, we can trust Him and His words. He Himself is the truth. We must travel with the Holy Spirit, who provides help and guidance for us. Jesus sent Him to us for our benefit. Many Christians have never allowed the Holy

Spirit to be a part of their life because they communicate only to the Father and the Son. All believers have the Holy Spirit; He goes before us and with us. But we often times don't pay Him any attention. The Holy Spirit is in this world now as the Father and Jesus are in heaven. Walk with Him and talk with Him like a friend.

There is nowhere else in this world that is safer than under God's wings, and of that I can be certain. In the U.S., there are many catastrophes - murders everywhere, shootings everywhere, even innocent people constantly being victims of crime. There is no safety anywhere but with the Lord - not even in churches, synagogues, or temples. Shootings are prevalent. Many physical places are no longer as safe- not even homes, cars, trains, or airplanes.

I've even witnessed on television a man who descended into a sinkhole while he was lying in bed in his bedroom. That's why I believe that only under His wings can we find true safety in this world. How much more would our Lord Jesus Christ protect His followers under His wings if a hen could do the same for her chicks? He is ready to take care of you. But are you ready to trust in Him? If so, do it with complete faith. Come running like those chicks under the Lord's wings. He is willing to hide you under His mighty wings. But again, I ask, are you willing to seek safety in the shelter of Jesus?

Moreover, please memorize Psalms 91 so that you can use it with faith in times of need. I've never memorized any of the Psalms. My justification for this was always that I am prone to forgetting things and, even in school, I didn't like to memorize things. After I turned the passage into my own Psalm by replacing "you" and "yours" with "I", "me", and "mine", I had a great desire to memorize it because I saw how I could use it in my life. When the Holy Spirit appears, He will teach us everything and refresh our memories about everything, as Jesus claimed in His words.

Thus, I prayed for the Holy Spirit to teach me, and now I wish to memorize everything.

I couldn't believe I had picked it up in just a few days. Now I am able to recite my own translation of Psalms 91 when I don't have time to read the Bible. I adore my prayer and declaration of faith, which is what my memorization of Scripture is. I had so much faith that I knew I could withstand COVID and the vaccine. Moreover, I memorized Psalms 1, 23, and 121 of the Bible in my native language. I think God was preparing me for my encounter with COVID. I give my Lord thanks and praise. I have shared all of these situations in order to strengthen your faith and trust in Jesus Christ and in His words. Fear cannot remain in your heart when faith in Jesus and His words come to you.

To fight evil, faith is very significant. Faith comes from God and fear comes from the devil. The one is just opposite from the other. Speak the words of faith. Let the adversary know of our faith in Jesus. If we give in to fear and unfavorable language our adversary will listen and he'll realize we have no means of stopping him or resisting him. That proves to him that we are unable to oppose him due to the fact that, as Ephesians chapter 6 states, faith is our shield. Always let the words of faith come out of your mouth.

Our tongues have the power to create life and death. Using positive words that are spoken in faith will give you life. Conversely, speaking negative words in despair or anger will bring about failure and strife. I think it's because our adversary hears these things and learns where we stand in order to take action against us. From today on, decide to live faith; speak life, speak faith, and count your blessings. Make a choice. to follow the truth of Jesus and resist the enemy's strategies with steadfastness. We must put our trust in Jesus. Always have a grateful heart.

Wearing the Weapon of War

Believers in Jesus Christ, put on the full armor of God as Saint Paul instructs in Ephesians Chapter 6 All of these 6 tools represent Jesus Himself.

1. The Helmet of Salvation mentioned in Ephesians 6:17 (NIV): "Take the helmet of salvation and the sword of the Spirit, which is the word of God…" We must make sure we are saved through Christ Jesus.

2. The breastplate of righteousness found in Ephesians 6:14 (NIV): "Stand firm then… with the breastplate of righteousness in place…" We are righteous because Jesus is righteous. We must act like Jesus. Do not look or act judgmentally, take sides in arguments just because of someone's status, or make rash

decisions.

3. The belt of truth mentioned in Ephesians 6:14(NIV): Stand firm then, with the belt of truth buckled around your waist." We must live according to the truth of Jesus and always speak His truth. I don't like being with lying people, therefore, I will stay away from them. Make sure not even a white lie comes from your mouth. Truth will give us confidence, and the truth will always win.

4. The sandals of peace mentioned in Ephesians 6:15 (NIV): "And with your feet fitted with the readiness that comes from the gospel of peace…" We must be peacemakers, not peace breakers. I also encourage you to bring the good news of peace to others. Jesus is the Prince of Peace.

5. The shield of faith mentioned in Ephesians 6:16 (NIV): "In addition to all this, take up the shield of faith, with which you can extinguish all the flaming arrows of the evil one." The best defense against the enemy is faith in Jesus and His teachings. Jesus used the Bible to defeat

Satan, and we can too. Even if we hold swords in both hands, without a shield, we can still be harmed.

6. The Sword of the Spirit mentioned in Ephesians 6:17 (NIV): "…the sword of the Spirit, which is the word of God." We have to walk with Jesus and we must have these tools of Jesus Christ in our lives.

Jesus is unable to stand by someone who lacks compassion, truth, righteousness, or peace. Saint Paul encourages us to be like Jesus Christ. "Rather, clothe yourselves with the Lord Jesus Christ, and do not think about how to gratify the desires of the flesh." (Romans 13:14, NIV).. By abiding in Christ, we become brand new creatures. We need to understand Jesus' character. We need to develop to be like Him. We first need to understand His nature or character. Where do we learn how to be that way from? We learn how to be like Him by studying and meditating on the word of God. We have heard "WWJD"—"What would Jesus do"? But I say "WWJS"--"What would Jesus say?"

We can also ask the Holy Spirit to teach us. He is the great instructor. His virtues, such as truth, justice, mercy, peace, compassion, etc., must guide us. If we embody His qualities, we are in harmony with God. Our adversaries are unable to accuse us of anything if we are in this alignment with God. The devil won't have anything to say against us. So, put on the armor of God and always hide yourself under His wings so that Satan cannot harm you.

Prepare yourself for the upcoming pandemic or anything else that may be on the way. Be steadfast in the Lord. Our Lord won't hand us over to our enemies. I sincerely hope and pray that the readers of this brief message will be encouraged. Instead of being afraid of the enemy, we want to have great faith in our Lord.

I have never thought about writing a book like this. I have personally witnessed this story to many people. But one day, it came to my mind to write down everything I'd learned in a book for the benefit of others since more hard times are ahead.

I requested of the Holy Spirit through prayer to stop me from publishing this book unless it was His will. He hasn't stopped me yet, and I hope that everyone who reads the Bible and believes in Jesus will get the revelations I've had in this book. Before the next hard time strikes, I hope people will take this story seriously and seek shelter under God's wings -- that is the only place we will all be safe. Please read and accept Proverbs 18:10 (NIV) as well: "The name of the Lord is a fortified tower; the righteous run to it and are safe."

The name of our Lord Jesus is, in fact, a tall tower. By holding fast to this verse, you can call upon His name when any kind of attack occurs. The adversary as a result must flee; he cannot stand hearing God's name. I have experienced the power of God's name, both in real life and once in a very disturbing dream. During these times, when I called upon the name of Jesus, the adversary backed off from me. In these circumstances, I didn't even bother to speak to the enemy. Instead, I called upon His name. Wow, what a lovely name that is! God has empowered us to use His name. Above all other names, the name of Jesus has the ability to protect us.

Prayer for the Believers (Readers) in Jesus' Name

Let me pray for you.

Dearest heavenly Father, I thank and praise you for allowing me to share the revelations you gave me with the world.

Lord, may the words included in this small book be a gift to all who read it. I have a lot of faith now because of these revelations that I have received from the Holy Spirit. May everyone who reads this book have confidence in the Lord Jesus Christ, that they will be protected under His wings like King David.

May the fear be driven out of their hearts and

their faith be strengthened. Let everyone who reads this book have the fortitude to tackle whatever comes their way in this world. Our high tower is you, Lord Jesus. Let everyone rush towards you. I give you thanks and praise for all that you have accomplished in our lives, especially for granting us the right to use your priceless, holy name. Equip your children to encourage others. In Jesus' name, I entrust these readers to you, and give you all the praise.

We are grateful that you have heard our prayers and given them loving attention. In Jesus' name I pray, amen.

Afterword

I am very grateful to my nephews, my nieces, and my children for helping me with my writing and computer work. More than anything else, I thank my Lord for enabling me to write down my life experience for the benefit of His children. He is great and mighty.

References to Verses Discussing "Hiding Under His Wings"

Psalms 91:1-4 (NIV)
"Whoever dwells in the shelter of the Most High will rest in the shadow of the Almighty. I will say of the Lord, "He is my refuge and my fortress, my God, in whom I trust." Surely he will save you from the fowler's snare and from the deadly pestilence. He will cover you with his feathers, and under his wings you will find refuge; His faithfulness will be your shield and rampart."

Psalms 63:7 (NIV)
"Because you are my help, I sing in the shadow of your wings."

Psalms 17:8-9 (NIV)
"Keep me as the apple of your eye; hide me

in the shadow of your wings from the wicked who are out to destroy me, from my mortal enemies who surround me."

Psalms 57:1 (NIV)
"Have mercy on me, my God, have mercy on me, for in you I take refuge. I will take refuge in the shadow of your wings until the disaster has passed."

Psalms 36:7 (NIV)
"How priceless is your unfailing love, O God! People take refuge in the shadow of your wings."

Psalms 61:4 (NIV)
"I long to dwell in your tent forever and take refuge in the shelter of your wings."

Ruth 2:12 (NIV)
"May the Lord repay you for what you have done. May you be richly rewarded by the Lord, the God of Israel, under whose wings you have come to take refuge."